THE HOLY APOSTLES

MATTHEW

<< The book of the generation of Jesus Christ the Son of David the Son of Abraham >>

<< In the beginning was the Word and the Word was with God and the Word was God >> JOHN

There was in the days of Herod the king of Judea, a certain priest named Zacharias of the division of Abijah, his wife...

LUKE

A voice of one shouting in the desert. Prepare the way of the Lord. Make His Path straight...

MARK

VISION OF GOD
AND THE FOUR CREATURES
CHERUBIM GUARDIANS OF THE
THRONE OF GOD
EZEKIEL 1:10

MA

T0368998

A prayer to the Virgin Mary
Through the intercessions of the Theotokos.
Savior save us.

Copyright © 2017 by Maria Athanasiou. 759486

ISBN: Softcover   978-1-5434-3231-2
       Hardcover   978-1-5434-3232-9
       EBook   978-1-5434-3626-6

Scripture quotations marked KJV are from the
Holy Bible, King James Version (Authorized
Version). First published in 1611. Quoted from
the KJV Classic Reference Bible, Copyright ©
1983 by The Zondervan Corporation.

Print information available on the last page

Rev. date: 07/15/2017

To order additional copies of this book, contact:
Xlibris
1-888-795-4274
www.Xlibris.com
Orders@Xlibris.com

CHRIST PANTOCRATOR

This book is dedicated to the glory of God.
All glory belongs to God Our Saviour, the Lord Jesus Christ!
Thank you for all the gifts.

By Him therefore let us offer the sacrifice of praise
to God continually, that is, the fruit of our lips, giving thanks to
His name. *Hebrews 13:15*

Acknowledgments
Please pray for the health and salvation
of those who helped with this book:
Hierodeacon Parthenios
Fr. Nicholas Soteropoulos
Dean Soteropoulos
Maria Athanasiou and family

Bibliography
The Bible (King James Version)
The Collected Lives of the Saints
The Oral Tradition of the Orthodox Church

Matthew the Apostle and Evangelist

Matthew the Galilean, also known as Levi, was the son of Alpheus and brother of the Apostle James of Alpheus. He was a tax collector working for the Romans when the Jews were under the rule of the Roman Empire. Saint Matthew while at work received his calling when Jesus came by and said to him, "Follow Me!" Immediately Matthew followed Jesus and left behind his sinful way of life. Jesus ate in Matthew's house with tax collectors and sinners. When criticized for that, He answered, "Those who are well have no need for a doctor but those who are sick".

Matthew was very close to Jesus, traveled with Him and became one of His twelve Apostles. He wrote the first of the four Gospels in Aramaic, the common Jewish language, later translated into Greek. The Gospel of Matthew shows that Jesus Christ is the incarnate Son of God, prophesied in the Old Testament, who did works only the Messiah could do.

After Pentecost, Saint Matthew with the grace of the Holy Spirit spread the good news of salvation in the name of Jesus, to the Jews in Palestine and in far away places. He died in Ethiopia, a martyr of Jesus Christ. His feast day is November 16.

Then Jesus answered and said unto her, "O woman, great is thy faith: be it unto thee even as thou wilt." And her daughter was made whole from that very hour. *Matthew 15:28*

SAINT
MATTHEW
THE
EVANGELIST

Mark the Apostle and Evangelist

Mark, also known as John Mark, was one of the 70 disciples of Jesus. John was his Jewish name. Mark was his Roman name. Barnabas, one of the 70 disciples, was his cousin and his mother was Maria.

It was in Mark's house that the Last Supper took place, and Mark was the boy (with the jug of water) that the disciples followed to find the Upper Room, according to tradition. It is also said that he was one of the servants who filled with water the jugs in the wedding of Cana that Jesus turned into wine.

Saint Mark traveled with Paul and Barnabas. He accompanied Peter to his far away travels and wrote the second Gospel that means good news (in Greek, Evangelion).

In his Gospel, Saint Mark tells about the many miracles of Jesus Christ showing the divine power of the Lord, that Christ is truly the Son of God, and also the Suffering Messiah.

There is a great reward for those who endure their suffering to the end. He traveled to teach the Holy Gospel in Cyrene, Libya, Egypt; and he made a Church in Alexandria. He died about AD 68 a martyr for Jesus Christ. His feast day is April 25.

And Jesus answered and said unto him, "What wilt thou that I should do unto thee?" The blind man said unto him, "Lord, that I might receive my sight." And Jesus said unto him, "Go thy way; thy faith hath made thee whole." And immediately he received his sight, and followed Jesus in the way. *Mark 10:51-52*

SAINT
MARK
THE
EVANGELIST

THE
BEGINNING
OF THE
GOSPEL
OF JESUS
CHRIST
THE SON
OF GOD

Luke the Apostle and Evangelist

*L*uke was a Gentile, born in Antioch. He was a Greek doctor, an artist and one of the 70 disciples of Jesus. He traveled with Paul and followed him in Rome. Saint Luke is the first icon painter. He first painted the Holy Image of the Virgin Mary and Jesus. He also painted the icons of Saints Peter and Paul as he saw them. After he finished the icons, he brought them to the Theotokos, and when she saw them, she approved them and prayed that the grace of her Son and God, Jesus, be on them. Iconography is a sacred art. The icons are the Gospel in color with pictures, like windows looking to heaven.

Saint Luke wrote the third Gospel in Greek and dedicated it to a Gentile named Theophilos. He emphasized the power of prayer, the inspirational work of the Holy Spirit and that "Emmanuel" is God with us.

Luke also wrote "The Acts of the Apostles". In that book, he tells how the Holy Spirit enlightened the Holy Apostles to spread the good news of salvation from Jerusalem to the whole world and throughout the Roman Empire. Luke lived to be 85. His feast day is October 18.

And he said unto Jesus, "Lord, remember me when Thou comest into Thy Kingdom." And Jesus said unto him, "Verily I say unto thee, Today shalt thou be with Me in Paradise." *Luke 23:42-43*

SAINT
LUKE
THE
EVANGELIST

John the Theologian, Apostle and Evangelist

*J*ohn, from Bethsaida of Galilee, was the younger son of Zebedee and Salome and the brother of James the Great. He was a fisherman and one of the 12 Apostles, the beloved disciple of Jesus Christ.

He was present on Mount Tabor at the transfiguration, at the raising from the dead of the daughter of Jairus and at the Agony of Jesus in the Garden. He followed the Lord even to the Cross and Jesus asked him to care for His All Holy Mother. John cared for the Theotokos in Jerusalem and in Ephesus. After her Dormition in Jerusalem, he traveled from Ephesus to teach the Gospel. He wrote the 4th Gospel and three Epistles and taught about love, the most important commandment of God.

When John was exiled, on the Island of Patmos, while praying, he saw the Lord in a vision, telling him to write the last book of the Bible, the Revelation of the end times, the Second Coming of Jesus and the victory of the Kingdom of God over evil. When John was 105, he asked his disciples to dig a grave in the shape of a cross and entered it alive after he prayed. The grave was empty the next day. His feast day is May 8.

The woman saith unto Him, "I know that Messias cometh, which is called Christ: when He is come, He will tell us all things." Jesus saith unto her, "I that speak unto thee am He." *John 4:25-26*

Peter the Apostle

*S*imon was a poor fisherman, fiery, impulsive and uneducated. He was born in Bethsaida, village of Galilee, the son of Jonas and the brother of Andrew. Jesus gave him the new name (Peter, in Greek Petros) that means rock. He was very close to the Lord and the leader of the 12. Peter with John and his brother James were present at the Transfiguration on Mount Tabor, the raising from the dead of the daughter of Jairus and the prayer of Jesus in the garden.

When the Jews arrested Jesus, Peter followed them into the court of Caiaphas, the high priest, and before the rooster crowed he denied three times that he knew Christ, because of fear. He repented for denying Jesus and cried when he looked at the face of Jesus who was standing close by. Jesus forgave him.

On Pentecost, Saint Peter, enlightened by the Holy Spirit, preached with zeal, and 3000 believed and were baptized Christians. This was the first Church in Jerusalem. Saint Peter traveled teaching the Word of God in Judea, Antioch, Asia and Rome and made a Church in Antioch. Saint Peter wrote two Epistles. He taught to be patient and submit to the earthly role in this life and prepare for the age to come. He died in Rome a martyr of Jesus in AD 68. His feast day is June 29.

And I say also unto thee, that thou art Peter, and upon this rock I will build My church; and the gates of Hades shall not prevail against it. And I will give unto thee the keys of the Kingdom of Heaven: and whatsoever thou shalt bind on earth shall be bound in Heaven: and whatsoever thou shalt loose on earth shall be loosed in Heaven. *Matthew 16:18-19*

The true rock is Christ Himself and His Church is built on the faithful confession of all.

SAINT
PETER

Paul the Apostle

Paul, known as Saul, was born in Tarsus of Asia Minor. His father was a Jewish Pharisee. Paul studied in Jerusalem and had a Jewish and a Roman citizenship.

He was persecuting the Christians, until one day, while he was on the road to Damascus, traveling from Jerusalem, he had a vision of Jesus Christ, suddenly appearing in a great light. Saul fell on the ground and was blinded.

The Lord said to him, "Saul, Saul, why do you persecute Me?" Paul changed immediately. For three days he prayed and fasted and by divine revelation, was led to Ananias who healed him and baptized him. Saint Paul began to teach about Jesus of Nazareth, the Messiah and Son of the living God and to spread the Christian faith with great zeal.

Saint Paul only saw Jesus after His resurrection. He was not one of the 12, but he is called an apostle and a leader of them, equal to the 12. He wrote the Epistles in the New Testament, instructing in faith, and taught that the Church is the Kingdom of Heaven on Earth.

He traveled to Greece and Rome and defended Jesus Christ, spreading His Gospel to the Nations. He spent the last two years of his life in Rome where he died a martyr for Jesus Christ during the reign of Nero. His feast day is June 29.

Rejoice evermore. Pray without ceasing. In everything give thanks: for this is the will of God in Christ Jesus concerning you. *1 Thessalonians 5:16-18*

✝ *The Holy Apostles*

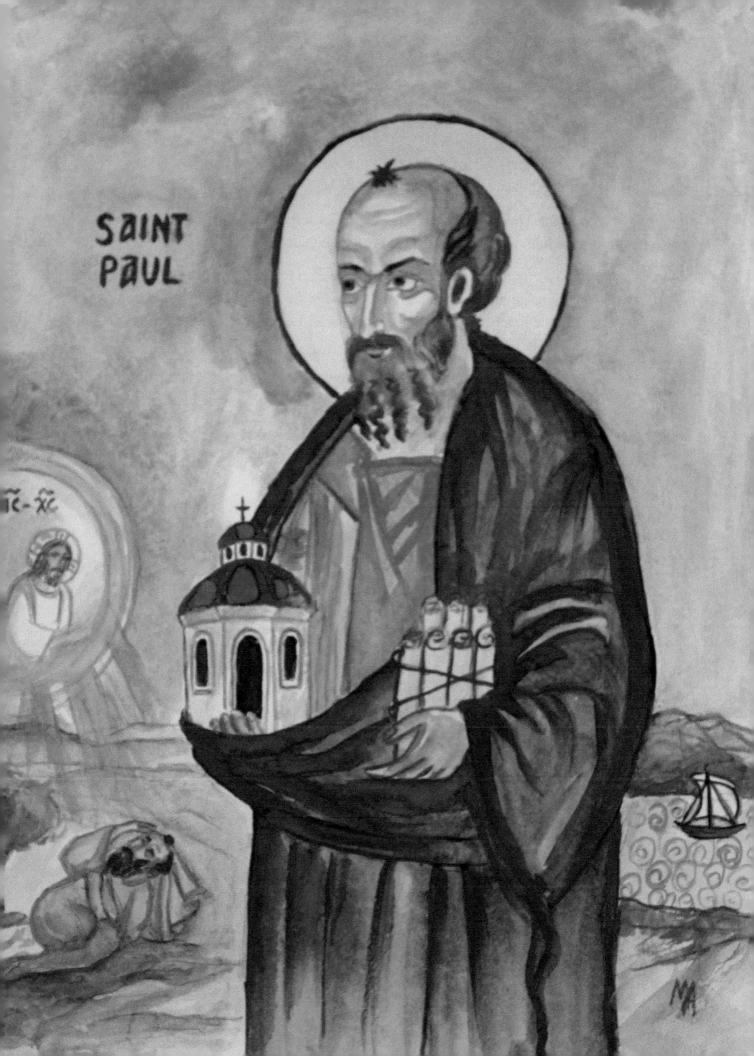

SAINT
PAUL

Andrew the First Called Apostle

*A**ndrew*** was the brother of Peter and the son of Jonas, born in Bethsaida of Galilee. He was a fisherman, the first called to be an Apostle of Jesus Christ.

Andrew with John the Theologian were students of John the Baptist, waiting for the Lord to come. Andrew, like John the Baptist, had long unkempt hair.

One day, as they were standing by the shore of the Jordan River, Jesus came; and when John the Baptist saw Him, he pointed to Him and said, "This is the Lamb of God who takes away the sin of the world." Immediately, Andrew followed Jesus and said, "We have found the Messiah."

After Pentecost, with the grace of the Holy Spirit, Andrew taught the Word of God and did many miracles. Once, in a port of Cyprus, after he blessed the ground, clear drinking water came running out. It is still running until today. Many believed and were baptized Christians.

When he healed Maximina from a sickness in the name of Jesus Christ, she believed and became a Christian. Her husband Galeatos of Patras crucified Andrew in an X-shaped Cross. The first letter of the name of Christ in Greek is X. This is the symbol of Saint Andrew. His holy remains are in Saint Andrew's Church in Patras. His feast day is November 30.

And there were certain Greeks among them that came up to worship at the feast: The same came therefore to Philip, which was of Bethsaida of Galilee, and desired him, saying, "Sir, we would see Jesus." Philip cometh and telleth Andrew: and again Andrew and Philip tell Jesus. And Jesus answered them, saying, "The hour is come, that the Son of Man should be glorified." *John 12:20-23*

Ὁ ἅγιος ἈΝΔΡἐας

"We have found the Messiah..."

MA

Thomas the Apostle

*T*homas, called Didymus, from Pansada of Galilee, was a fisherman, devoted to reading the Holy Scriptures. He knew so well the Word of God that when he heard about Jesus Christ, immediately he recognized Him as the Messiah and Savior, which the Prophets spoke about, and left his boat and followed Him. He became one of His Twelve Apostles.

Thomas was not in the Upper Room when Jesus appeared to His disciples, after His Resurrection. When the disciples told Thomas that they saw Jesus, he did not believe them. He said, "Unless I see with my own eyes, I cannot believe".

The following Sunday, when Jesus appeared again, Saint Thomas was there and saw Him. He then cried out, "My Lord and my God." Jesus told Thomas that more blessed is he who does not see and yet believes.

When the Theotokos was about to die, the Apostles were caught up in the clouds by Angels and were brought to her house. They buried her near Gethsemane. Saint Thomas arrived late; he asked the others about her body, but her tomb was found empty. Then Thomas saw her ascending in the clouds, and she gave him her belt. Thomas taught the Church that the Theotokos ascended into heaven bodily. Thomas returned to India to teach the Gospel of Christ. He died a Martyr's death. His relics are in Mount Athos and India. His feast day is October 6.

Thomas saith unto Him, "Lord, we know not whither Thou goest; and how can we know the way?" Jesus saith unto him, "I am the way, the truth, and the life: no man cometh unto the Father, but by Me." *John 14:5-6*

✝ *The Holy Apostles*

James the Brother of Jesus

*J*ames the Brother of Jesus, Adelphotheos in Greek, James the Just, James the Less, or Brother of God was a Nazarene, the son of Joseph the Betrothed with his first wife. Since a young age, he was devoted to God, lived a holy life and always studied the Holy Scriptures. From the start, he believed in the Lord Jesus. He called himself a bondservant of God and was one of the 70.

James was elected to be the First Bishop of Jerusalem. He served for 30 years. He wrote an Epistle in Greek to strengthen the Jewish and Gentile Christians. He also composed the first Liturgy, which Saint Basil and Saint John Chrysostom later used as their basis for writing their Liturgies of the Orthodox Church. He encouraged all to do works of faith. He said that faith without works is dead, just as the body without the spirit is dead, and that a prayer of faith will save the sick.

With his teachings many believed and were baptized Christians. The Pharisees and the Scribes did not like him and plotted to kill him. They threw him from the roof of the Jerusalem Temple. Before he died, he prayed to God to forgive them. He died in the year AD 63. His feast day is on the Sunday after Christmas.

Is any sick among you? Let him call for the elders of the church; and let them pray over him, anointing him with oil in the name of the Lord: And the prayer of faith shall save the sick, and the Lord shall raise him up; and if he have committed sins, they shall be forgiven him. *James 5:14-15*

Ὁ Ἅγιος Ἰάκωβος ὁ ἀδελφόθεος

James the Great, Brother of John the Theologian

James the Great, or James the Elder, was the older brother of John the Theologian, and son of Zebedee and Salome. Zebedee was a successful fisherman, and Salome a pious follower of Jesus Christ.

James and John were working on their father's boat when Jesus walked by the Sea of Galilee and called them. They immediately left their father and followed Jesus Christ. James was one of the 12 Apostles. James, his brother John and Peter were chosen by the Lord to be present and witness His Transfiguration on Mount Tabor, the miracle of the raising from the dead of the daughter of Jairus, and the agony of Jesus in the Garden of Gethsemane before His suffering in Golgotha.

After Pentecost, James, enlightened by the Holy Spirit, traveled far to preach about the Lord Jesus, the only true God, the Messiah. He went to Spain and other lands to teach. Many were baptized Christians.

The Pharisees and the Scribes did not like James because he fought them for their unbelief and hardness of heart. They sentenced him to death but that did not stop James. He remained calm and continued to teach about Jesus until his last breath. Saint James was a martyr. He died in Jerusalem at AD 44. His feast day is April 30.

> And when He had gone a little farther thence, He saw James the son of Zebedee, and John his brother, who also were in the ship mending their nets. And straightway He called them: and they left their father Zebedee in the ship with the hired servants, and went after Him. *Mark 1:19-20*

✝ *The Holy Apostles*

SAINT

JAMES
SON OF
ZEBEDEE

Stephen the Holy Protomartyr
and Archdeacon

*S*tephen, in Greek Stephanos, translated Crown, was a Greek Jew. He was a student of Gamaliel. His relative Saul, later known as Saint Paul, had the same teacher. According to the Acts, he was one of the seven deacons of the first Church in Jerusalem. The Apostles chose him to oversee the common tables of the brethren and give alms to the poor. Stephen was the eldest, therefore the Archdeacon.

He had theological knowledge, many virtues and unshakable faith. He was blessed with the gift of speaking well and performing miracles. He healed many sick in the name of the Lord Jesus Christ and was devoted to study the Holy Scriptures. He knew them exceedingly well.

He was arrested and brought in front of the Elders to apologize but instead of apologizing, he fearlessly spoke against the Jews and accused them for the murder of Jesus Christ. This angered the Jews very much. They dragged Stephen outside the gate and stoned him to death. The Virgin Mary and Saint John the Theologian were there, watching from a distance.

Before Stephanos died, he asked God to forgive his enemies. He was the first martyr that defended with his life the Church of Jesus. His feast day is December 27.

> But he, being full of the Holy Ghost, looked up steadfastly into Heaven, and saw the glory of God, and Jesus standing on the right hand of God. And said, Behold, I see the Heavens opened, and the Son of Man standing on the right hand of God. *Acts 7:55-56*

THE MARTYRDOM OF SAINT STEPHEN

SAUL THE EXECUTOR

MA

✝ *The Holy Apostles*

Dionysios Areopagitis the Hieromartyr

*D*ionysios was born in Athens from pagan parents. He studied philosophy and was a member of the Areospagus, the highest court in Greece. When Saint Paul went to the Areospagus, where the statue of the unknown God was, he asked Dionysios who that God was. Dionysios replied, "The One who will reign over all heaven and earth." Paul taught Dionysios the true God.

During the Crucifixion of Jesus, Dionysios saw the sun darkened and thought this was the end of the world. He was baptized Orthodox and left his family to accompany Paul on his missionary travels. Dionysios became the Bishop of Athens and had the gift of working miracles. He traveled to Jerusalem to meet the Mother of God and wrote a book about that visit. He described the Theotokos saying that he was amazed by the beauty of her soul and her resemblance to her Son Jesus. He also wrote a book about the Angels.

When he was 96, during the Christian persecution, under the reign of Emperor Domitian, he was arrested with his disciples and was tortured, but he was divinely protected. When they put him in jail, he chanted the Divine Liturgy. Jesus visited him with a host of angels. He was a martyr for Jesus Christ. Many miracles occurred at his grave. His feast day is October 3.

So Paul departed from among them. Howbeit certain men clave unto him, and believed: among the which was Dionysius the Areopagite, and a woman named Damaris, and others with them. *Acts 17:33-34*

εἰ ἅγιος ΔΙΟΝΥΣΙΟ ὁ ἈΡΕΟΠΑΓΙΤΗΣ

The Unknown God

ΝΑ

Οἱ Ἅγιοι ΠΆΝΤΕϹ

SUNDAY OF ALL THE SAINTS

Printed in the United States
by Baker & Taylor Publisher Services